ROMANTIC AND SEX POETRY

ANDREA FRIERSON

Made with ❤ on the Notion Press Platform
www.notionpress.com

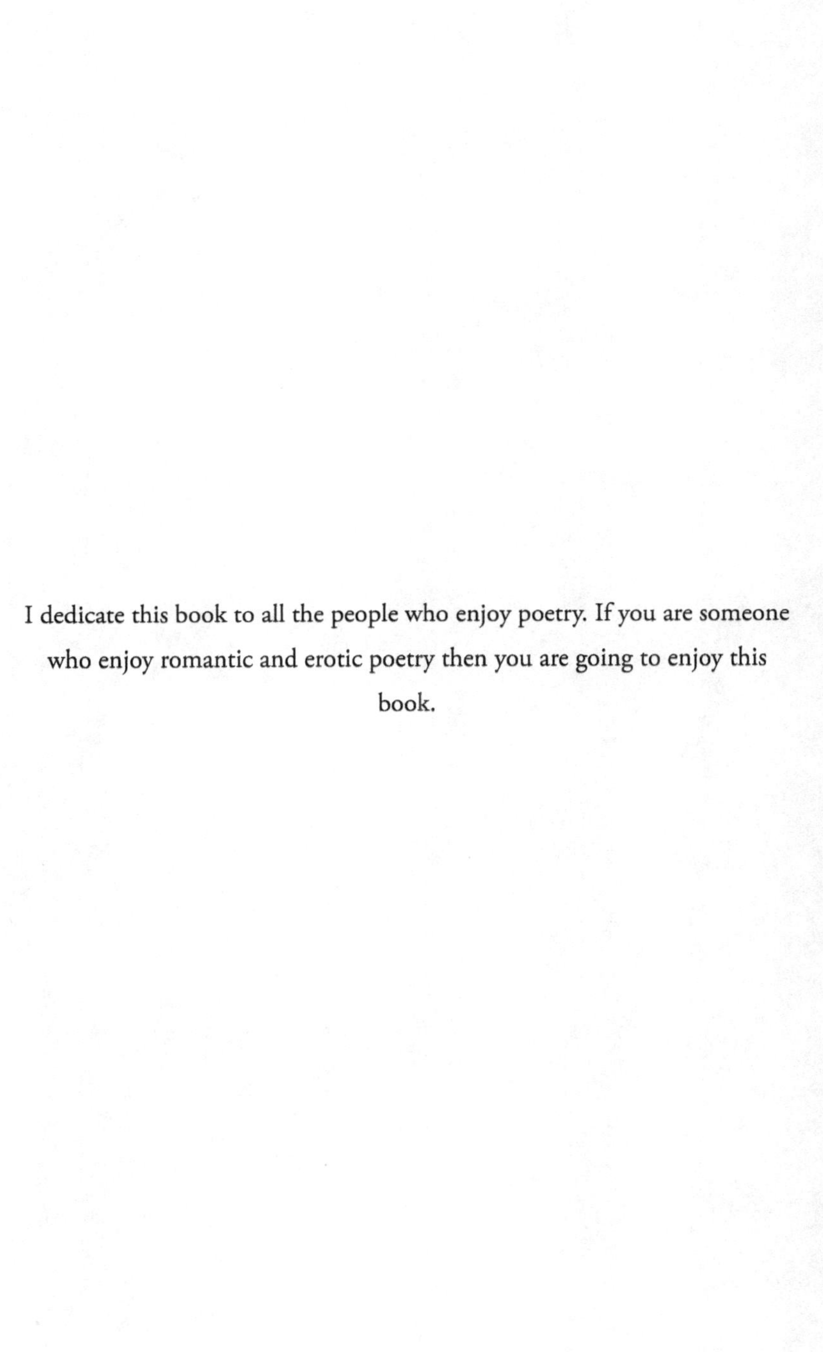

I dedicate this book to all the people who enjoy poetry. If you are someone who enjoy romantic and erotic poetry then you are going to enjoy this book.

Contents

Preface

My poetry comes from the heart and experience I've had. I also base it off of others I known in the past as well. I think poetry helps open me up and express myself in many ways. I hope you will give this book a chance to do the same for you.

Acknowledgements

I just want to say people around me and other authors out there thanks for inspiring me to write and continue on the path that I want to be on. This has truly been an experience for me and I appreciate it.

Prologue

This is just a poetry book full of fun poems. It consists of romantic and erotic type of poetry. I hope you read and enjoy.

Romantic Poetry

Poem 1

As he enter my body my soul begins to leave. I like how he feels when he deep in me. I shiver as my legs begin to shake. My body is feeling like an earthquake. The softness of his lips as I taste. The wetness between my legs without no trace. Panties on the floor silk lace. I'm on top as my body penetrates. I can't let go no ending early or letting great sex go to waste.

Poem 2

Pretty me looking for hansome you. Where did you go my boo? You into me I'm into you so what is it we have to lose. Kissing you is not like kissing another. The lips pressed against each other. The tongue lies but never tells so you say. We both can't wait to go on this magical date. There's no other way but for you to stay. I have freaky thoughts going every direction and each way.

Poem 3

Lick me like icecream I'm sweet as can be. There's no candy in the world sweet as me. I'm drippy not sticky so no worrying when it comes to me. I'll melt in your mouth and have you thinking you drinking sweet tea. Can you handle me there's no denying how great I can be. I don't give strokes but hear attacks might come to be.

Poem 4

I love the way you look at me it's like staring at stars in the deep sea. You complete me when you hold me and wrap your arms around while listening to the sea. As I whisper in your ear your mines to eat. You spread your legs wide as if the buffet is open to eat. I like to touch and caress every part of your meat. The dinner is for me to enjoy every little bite. As you scream my name leaving love bites.

Poem 5

I'm shaped like a coke bottle waiting for you to swallow. I'm like soda waiting to explode not for you to hold my hand. Do you like how I taste and no time to waste any of me. I don't do no smashing but romance I can. I'm like a love song that you always walking around humming. You like a tall glas of milk that does me no wrong.

Poem 6

Sexy sounds as you make while I'm inside of you. Deep long strokes which takes control of you. I lick here and there everywhere as I'm deep in you. I'm taking your body to another level which completes you. Your body begins to shake as if an earthquake taken over you. Let the rivers from your body overflow and take over you. I like it really wet as I drown in you. There's no life left in me as I take control of you.

Poem 7

Strawberries and cherries when I think of you. I want to play with you in my mouth and tickle you. I use my tongue to cuddle next to you. You hang down low just enough for me to please you. You laugh as my tongue play and tickle you. You say stop but keep going is what I want to do to you. As your juices run down on my chin as I'm eating you.

Poem 8

I'm his gift and he's ready to open me up. I want him to be suprised of
what's inside. There's no reason to act shy or hide. I'm more like a special
gift not easy on the eyes. When think of me you think of chocolate covered
up but it's not a candy bar inside. I can run a man crazy when he's finally on
the inside. There's no strings tighter than my wet insides.

Poem 9

I'm more than just a situation and can't just go away. You played with my
heart and threw it away. I dare you come back and try to repair. Do you
think about all times you played and all girls you'd share. I'm a mess and I
know it because I can't just ignore it. As mad as I am this knife I can't just
throw it. It's a suicide within inside of me and me steady begging for a plea.
Why didn't you love me? I guess now you realize you needed me.

Poem 10

It's long and strong standing straight up. I do want to put my lips on it as
the nut come up. My lips are soft so you can enjoy the feel. I want to caress
the top of it as it spills. The white on top tastes so sweet. I'm going to need
more of this dessert as I use no teeth. My tummy is full of your love as it
pours into my mouth. This is one tastey feeling and one of the best desires.

Poem 11

Beautiful eyes staring into my face. I like how you stand when you are in
my space. I aim to please and never the one to tease. I like when getting
pleased when you down on your knees. I feel the wetness from your mouth

satisfying my needs. I like it hard and strong touching me deep inside and gets me sprung. Your love is enough for me no need no satisfactory from no other but me.

Poem 12

Chocolate all over me and all over you. There's so many yummy things I would like to do. I want to taste the flavor on my mouth and for you to use your tongue down south. My ocean is full and white as the sea. I know you going to enjoy every moment exploring me. I know you want to let your tongue wonder until it get lost inside of me.

Poem 13

My juices all over your mouth from tasting you down south. I meal I can really enjoy and no toying around just want to explore. Slide up in me with want to feel it deep within in me. Moans from my sweet voice which penetrates me. My juices running down your legs as you go back in fourth in me. I like when you aim to satisfy and take care of me.

Poem 14

I like long wals on the beach while letting water wet my feet. I'm enjoying the cool breeze with you next to me. I like for us to hold hands as we walk and speak. We gaze into each other's eyes as began to laugh. I like fun and good time we always known to have. Love never leave us that's what I tell myself. I want to be with you forever as I enjoy myself.

Poem 15

Beautiful round and large. You come in such sizes. Beautiful round and large come with so many suprises. Beautiful round and large make me want to just bite them. Beautiful round and large you know how to excite me. I'm so soft make you just want to bite me. Suck on me all night until I get sore. You can even rub and massage me making me want more.

Poem 16

A broken heart one must face the lost can never be replaced. I cry tears that spill from the eyes to cheek which never dissapear. I'm all a lone hoping and praying you will come home. I write a love letter to the music but really it's no song. I'm saddened by love which I thought I belong. I never in a million years though I would end up a lone.

Poem 17

Walk and hold my hands and never let me go. Spend time with me and cuddle up and don't have me just for show. I want to be spoiled and treated like a queen. I'm not used to getting ignored and not recieving things. It's about what's on the inside you always tell me. You can't see the heart physically but emotionally you can feel me.

Poem 18

Lips soft as yours I want to kiss all the time. I want to caress them all day while massaging mine. I don't mind the extra slob just make it even wetter. I know you going to do a great job while kissing me even better. I leave no traces that's why I wear no lipstick. The smell of your long dick touching my lips on the tip.

Poem 19

As you fuck me my legs began to trimble. I have wetness of white inbetween my legs. I'm shaking wanting to taste that nice round head. I want to enjoy every moment of pleasing you. Sometimes I get joy out of teasing you. Do you like when I suck all over you? I want a mouth full of greatness so you make all my dreams come true. I'm nasty and you love it. There's no complaining or getting over it.

Poem 20

He lays next to me staring into my eyes. I look at him with guilt and plea hoping he will smile. There's betrayal and love lost with no coming back. I just want him to grip me or rub my back. What did I do to deserve this? I took a chance with a risk. Tears running down my eyes as I feel selfish. If only I could change times and could take back this.